33 Fiverr Gigs That Sell Like Crazy!

Featuring proven job ideas used by top sellers.

Check out more recent titles from us

33 Fiverr Power Tips

Power Profits! Cash Flow Revolution

**63 Ways to DRIVE MORE TRAFFIC
to your website**

**101 TOTALLY FREE ways
to market your website or blog**

How To Build a YouTube Money Machine

The 10 Principles of ENDLESS WEALTH

About the author

Danial Barron Howe is the author of over 350 books ranging from business and online income to health and wellness. He is the founder of six multinational businesses including **2ndEmpireMedia**, the publisher of this book and FiverrPowerTips.Com**,** a rapidly growing community catering to the ongoing education of the Fiverr community.

Dan has been involved in the information marketing business ever since he wrote his first book, ***POWER PROFITS!*** Nearly a decade and a half ago. Since that time he has gone on to sell over 750,000 books in both printed and electronic form as well as numerous audio, video and other hybrid forms of informational products.

In addition to his role as an informational product producer, he holds several degrees including a Masters in mechanical engineering and design as well as degrees in psychology and biomechanics. He is a lifelong tinkerer artist and visionary innovator with a passion for improving efficiencies of systems such as those found within this book.

Forward

Why would anyone get so excited about earning *five bucks*?
By now you have probably noticed that the Internet tends to pop up every year with another new idea on how to promote your website or make easy money. The latest "new idea" seems to be a trend towards ***micro job sites***. Several of these new sites have popped up in recent years but only one among them reigns truly supreme above all others – **Fiverr.com**

Founded in 2010, Fiverr is the 800 pound gorilla of micro job sites. In little more than a years time it seems to have come out of nowhere and exploded all over the net. At the time of this writing fiverrs membership is 20 million strong and growing with as many as 5000 new jobs being added daily.

Should you get involved with fiverr?
Yes! With a membership pool this deep (and getting deeper every day) that represents a *gold mine* of unlimited opportunity just waiting to be harvested. It should be noted however as well that there are two major differences between a successful fiverr seller and one who fails*:*

1. The successful seller has learned how to identify a "*winning*" buyer group with a recurring user base.
2. The successful seller also has a streamlined system (based on templates) to get his work done in the fastest, most efficient way, *often in only a few minutes.*

I can't develop your listings for you, nor can I market them for you. What I *will do* is teach you how to discover winning gig ideas and get good at driving traffic to your sales pages. *Very, very good…* This above all else is what will separate you from those that never seem to seen any attention, despite having otherwise very marketable ideas.

Why most how-to books are out-of-date before they are ever written even published.
A lot of "*how to*" books are written by folks who got out of the business more than half a decade ago (marketing of any type is always changing and you need to stay on the cutting edge.) or by academics who believe they understand the "mechanics" of a business enough to teach others. Sadly, most do not!

Still, others are make it only because of the number of personal contacts in their *Rolodex*. These are the ones that tell you how they made a million dollars using their "*XYZ 3 step automatic plan*".

Oh, if it were only that simple! These old ideas won't work on Fiverr.

I am a full-time information marketer.
Let me be clear upfront; I am not going to fill your head full of theoretical nonsense or recycled gibberish that I've pulled from various places all over the Internet. *I am a full time professional information marketer and TOP RATED Fiverr user*. I'm in the trenches each day earning a living by the knowledge that I've acquired over a decade and a half of actual use. I have to, this is how I feed myself and my family!

… And now for a shameless marketing plug:

Although the information in this book will take you a long, long way in the understanding of setting up your own personal Fiverr sales machine, the tips found here are only a few of the many tools available to you and you should always be on the lookout for more. You wouldn't expect to build a house using just one hammer would you?

When you're ready to take your Fiverr sales to the next level, I've put together a virtual toolbox of Fiverr resources for you on my website. Inside you'll find:

- *Plug-and-play sales pages- All you need to do is just fill in your specific gig information and drop it into your fiverr sale page.*
- *You'll get the very same templates I use to lay out my sales with - You'll also be able to develop original, marketable & hugely profitable e-books for sale on fiverr, amazon and more in a matter of hours - not weeks or months.*
- *...and I'll even show you how to set up a fully functional website using a free development software package that comes complete with shopping cart, photo gallery and advanced tools!*

For more details on this product and many more, visit my site at:

www.FiverrPowerTips.Com

Index

Preface

What does it takes to make a living online?
When you look at the statistics for failed business startups the prospects are pretty dismal.
Why do so many fail? Generally the answer falls into three categories:

1. They are inadequately funded
2. The owners lack an essential skill or knowledge (or at the very least a workable plan)
3. But the biggest is *loss of motivation…* This happens a lot in the informational marketing business. And the same goes for Fiverr as well.

The good news is that gaining traffic for your fiverr sales does not have to take a huge upfront investment of cash or really even much effort either. It can be grown step-by-step-as I have done – and I will show you the best of everything I know right here in this book.

British Prime Minister Winston Churchill, famously addressed a graduating class. When asked to speak he stood up, walked to the podium, quietly surveyed the crowd in attendance and instead of delivering an expectedly long winded speech, he simply announced *"Never give up! Never give up! **Never <u>ever</u> give up!"*** and with that he returned to his seat…. nuff said.

Building a sustainable business on Fiverr is a numbers game.
It may come across as obvious to many of you, but understanding this fact is the key to success. The misunderstanding many beginners have is to expect to create *a single gig* that will produce a flood of traffic

year after year, and that thinking won't get you very far.

To be a successful you must have *many promotional hooks in the water* at any given time. Fiverr allows you to post a maximum of 20 gigs, and successful sellers know how to take advantage of all of them. Some will make you a little bit of money, while others could make you a lot!

The reality is that if you only put up a couple of gigs on Fiverr and expect the traffic to beat a path to your door you're going to come away sorely disappointed. As mentioned earlier, Fiverr is growing by leaps and bounds and its user base is currently in the millions. However, there's only so much room on the top page to be a featured seller. If you're not on that page it's unlikely anyone will ever know you exist. This presents a problem; *how will the buyers find you?* The answer rests solely on the actions that you take to actively promote your gigs on your own.

Relax, everything you need to succeed is already at hand.
Promotion of any kind isn't rocket science. You are simply finding relevant groups of interested people and letting them know where to find you (or maybe just making your first introduction.

Let me assure you that you don't need a sparkling personality or outstanding speaking skills. (Even when it comes time to make your promotional video) Heck, you don't honestly need the looks of a Hollywood actor and you really don't even need a great education. I've seen several successful examples of this theory all over fiverr! All you need to do is a little one time work to develop a well laid out, organized presentation and know how to deliver it in the most effective manner.

What DO you need most to be successful?
Volume! As I said before, success with Fiverr is a numbers game. The more you put yourself out there, the closer you come to greater and greater success as a seller. Don't worry, you WILL get there, but I won't try to kid you and tell you that it doesn't take an investment of your time and effort up front to get things moving. But, just picture yourself sitting on a tropical beach while the rest of the world deposits automatic money into your account from sales you made online. People do a lot more difficult things all over this Earth every day for the sake of a "job".

*(No doubt you've heard this "dream scenario" many times before but I can tell you **this is my reality!** Internet marketing has allowed me to move from America to an island paradise in the Philippines. As I sit here dictating this book I'm on the back deck of my house overlooking the ocean. Rough life eh?)*

What if I do something wrong or nobody buys anything?
Don't worry, you'll screw up and you'll probably get involved in many unproductive activities more than once that will make you will want to quit and lick your wounds. It's happened to the best of us. Here's my best advice; *Get over yourself!* This is a learning process and nobody learns by succeeding all the time. If you picked the wrong gig offer, designed a horrible looking pitch page, or just lacked the confidence it takes to make a well presented audio or video, learn from it! Make the appropriate adjustments and then move on. Don't give up.

My secret:
Do you want to know a secret that few beginning Fiverr promoters recognize when faced with a situation like this? We live in the digital age. NOTHING ONLINE IS

PERMANENT. Corrections can be made with just a few keystrokes and the click of a mouse. And you can always update or tweak your offer as many times as you want. New potential visitors will never know how bad things used to be.

Really, every time you develop a new gig offer you are beginning with a clean slate. Once you have learned the basics, then you'll have a *template* to work from. The truth; is there is no reason to be embarrassed or worry about ruining your reputation. Unless you are a well-known celebrity most visitors to your sale page could care less who you are, as long as what you're providing is of sufficient value to them.

The biggest mistake you can make.
The truth is; not every gig on Fiverr is worth a damn. No matter how amazing you may believe your offer is, or how snazzy the promotional video or associated photos look or even how slick your pitch is. Bottom line: Fiverr buyers vote with their wallets. If you're not making sales the problem is something you're doing is not resonating with buyers and if you fail to address this fact you will never hit the big time.

Often times fiverr sellers with no formal promotional skills jump headlong into ideas that they *think* the public would be interested in, never doing even the least little bit of research to find out if there *actually even is* a market. My advice here is simple: proceed slowly. Test things out with a few promotions (you have nothing to lose - it's always free to post your gigs) and see what kind of traffic comes of it before getting crazy and going all out.

The greatest system of the 21st century.

Throughout the course of my life I have been involved in many, many different enterprises. I have been a real estate investor, television producer, professional motorcycle manufacturer, and a whole host of other things. Each business came with its benefits and drawbacks however, few ever provided me the free time to actually enjoy my life the way marketing informational products has. The internet has truly revolutionized the way business can be done – *but if and only if you learn the rules first!*

I can say without a doubt that developing informational products and services and then marketing them through my various sales channels such as my websites, blogs, Youtube videos and yes, even fiverr as well has been an ongoing challenge and a thrill for me.

Sure, there was a learning curve with all of it, there always is. But, once I crossed that threshold into knowledge and proficiency I was able to enjoy a lifestyle that few will ever able to experience.

If you desire a life filled with more free time, the ability to apply your creativity in myriads of ways and a potentially far better rate of pay then you're currently earning, remember the words of Winston Churchill; *"Never give up! Never give up! Never, ever give up!"*

Ready? Then let's get started!

#1 Logo Design

One of the simplest ways to make money on fiverr is to apply a little artistic creativity. Not everybody is naturally artistic or has an eye for graphically pleasing layout so this represents a tremendous opportunity for those of you who do.

One of the most popular creative gigs in this niche is logo design. There is never a time when this service is not needed. There are always new companies, organizations or causes that need a visual representation and for just a few bucks invested in some quality software (or you may already have something), you could have a nonstop pool of clientele to draw from.

How to get started:
Grab a copy of one of the better graphic illustration software packages out there. You don't need to go with the latest & most expensive one either. There's nothing wrong with owning a software package that's a few versions older (especially since you can pick them up for dirt cheap and they still do the job! - I'm still using Adobe InDesign 2.0 and I have no reason to upgrade because it still serves me quite well.)

If you are going to be serious about doing graphic work you can't use the free market software that came with your computer, it's simply not up to the task. Here are a few of the better packages I would suggest:

- Corel design
- Adobe InDesign

- Adobe Illustrator

Build a mini portfolio.
Once you get your software installed, spend some time playing with it. One of the best uses of your practice time is creating a mini portfolio of your work to show your prospective clients. Buyers are unlikely to purchase from you unless they can see the type of work you're capable of so this is time well spent.

Once you get a collection of 10 or so top-quality examples, post them on your sale page, write up a good description of what you're offering and you're ready to roll.

How to set yourself apart from other sellers
Instead of merely offering the basic logo design why not offer

- business card layouts
- letterhead layouts
- large-format scalable vector graphics (these could be used for storefront applications)
- or you could consider offering *two or three logo possibilities for the price of one* - I'm a big fan of this technique because it really does set you apart from the average seller. You'll see me make this suggestion all throughout the book because it provides outrageous value and buyers respond to it!

#2 Voice Overs

If you were lucky enough to be born with the right "pipes" why not put them to good use? There are so many opportunities for voiceovers on fiver it just boggles the mind. Here's a few of the top sellers:

- Product voice overs

- Prerecorded phone messages

- Message while on hold recordings (for corporate use)

- Impersonations – If you are really good at impersonating a pop culture icon or well-known celeb you can make a killing at this one.

How to get started:

You don't need much cash outlay for this one. The only real requirement is a quality microphone. My personal favorite is the **Xoom microphone** - it runs about $200 bucks and creates truly professional quality audio in just about every environment. The best part about it is you don't have to be chained to a computer to use it. Once you get your recording done you can upload it to your computer and process it as needed.

It looks a lot more high-tech than it really is, after playing with it for about five minutes you haven't figured out and you can record some amazing audio with it.

I would also advise you grab a copy of one of the freely available *audio editors* that can be found on the web as well so you can clean things up before you submit them to your client.
One of the best for the job is *audacity*.

The poor man's sound booth

I want to share a personal funny story about resourcefulness that I'm sure those who you that are on a limited budget will appreciate.

Years ago some friends of mine and I had the idea to host an event in Vegas at a well-known casino to promote one of my businesses. It was a massive undertaking, and one that stretched our collective budgets well past all reasonable limits.

In order to promote the event we were going to need to make a commercial - a hugely expensive undertaking if you want to do it right. But time was ticking and we didn't have the luxury of waiting or saving up - let alone any credit left on our cards to pull it off.

Luckily one of my friends just happened to be blessed with a voice that you would swear was *custom made* for the job. I got the crazy idea to create a sound booth in the bathroom of our hotel. If you know anything about audio reproduction this choice is quite possibly the *worst* imaginable location to record anything due to the echoes created from the tiny space and abundance of hard surfaces.

After hearing the first *dry run* it sounded horrible! It was tinny sounding and full of echoes and it sounded like he is broadcasting from inside a soda can! … So what to do?

A solution was had in the form of thick blankets and sheets hung all over the bathroom to deaden the sound. We quickly *short sheeted* the beds in the room and padded every inch of the bathroom we could using duct tape and gaffers clips to hold everything in place while my friend literally sat in the tub with his script to record round 2 of my inspired insanity.

If the maids would have popped in and discovered us while coming in to clean during our impromptu "recording session" they would have been scratching their heads for weeks trying to figure out what the hell we were doing!

Did it work? You be the judge.

Listen to the result here
http://bit.do/did-it-work

Pleased with the results, I knew that the rest of the acoustic issues would be masked by the soundtrack I would layer over the voice overs.

The final product
http://bit.do/final-product

Wallah! Low buck audio magic!

The big take away here is that with a little effort and determination you CAN get the job done. Big budgets don't always solve every problem. Put together your own low buck studio and go out there and claim your share of the huge number of clients on fiverr looking for voice talent.

For those that want to know how the story ends. We went on to hold our seminar grossing over $685,000 after expenses. It was a life changing experience for all of us.

#3 Video Testimony

Audio testimonies are hot sellers on fiverr, but video testimonies are *even hotter*! Before you get the idea that you need to be a Hollywood actor or have model good looks to pull this off, let me be the first to tell you that that's simply not the case. There's plenty of room in the video testimony segment for the "average Joe" to make some great money.

Video testimonies are commonly used by information marketers and small companies looking to make a name for themselves or their latest product. Fiverr represents a *massive bargain* for this type of client (and there's no shortage of them) because they don't have to spend time searching out talent and setting up all the logistics of filming everything - that's your job.

Typically video testimony sellers require their clients to provide them a script of 30 seconds to a minute with a set number of words (and of course they offer *up sells* with *gig extras* if the client wants more)

How to get started:
Depending upon the type of video you're offering your investment can be cheap or quite expensive. A typical man on the street type video can be shot with an average camcorder (Don't use your cell phone. I don't care how good you think it is, it's still not good enough!)

At the very least you need a camcorder with a quality microphone (and for my sake, please use a tripod to avoid shaky looking video, jittery cam work drives me nuts!). From there the sky is the limit. Of course there's always something you can add that will make things better, but the challenge is knowing when enough is enough.

No doubt about it, producing acceptable video is substantially more complex than audio. There's many things to be taken into consideration such as:

- Lighting
- Camera equipment
- Background
- Props
- Set
- and yes, *quality audio* still plays a part - you don't want to provide a video with terrible audio because your client will definitely leave you bad feedback if his message can't be understood or viewers have to struggle to understand what's being said.

I would highly suggest you do a couple of demo clips for your gig to show your potential clients what kind of quality you will be providing. A couple of tips to look out for here is to make sure that you are well lit with no obvious shadows anywhere and that you can be heard clearly without any echoes or wind noise.

In addition, speak clearly look at the camera and maintain a pleasant, enthusiastic disposition. This will go a long way and selling yourself to a client.

How to set yourself apart from other sellers

- offer longer videos that his competitors or more words in the script

- offer special backgrounds

- offer multiple videos for the same basic price (2 for 1 or even 3 for 1)

- offer special outfits (professional suit, casual, ethnic or sexy attire)

Side note:

Remember, it's going to be your face that's going on the final product and it's going to be out there on the web for a long, long time. If you don't feel comfortable associating your image with a product or representing something then you have the right to say "no".

That being said, it's best to set *ground rules* with your buyers *before* getting started. If there's a limit to what you will do make sure that's made clear to your buyer upfront. You'd be surprised by some of the requests you will get if you don't!

#4 Written Product Reviews

In my opinion *everybody* selling on fiver should have this gig as part of their repertoire because it's the easiest money you'll ever make on fiverr.

There is absolutely *no limit* to the amount of sales you can make with this gig and everyone stands an equal chance to make exceptional money at this because there are always book authors and product sellers looking for reviews on their latest offerings in places such as Amazon.com, good reads, smashwords and more.

In addition to eBooks there's also a strong market for reviews of physical products you can do as well, and we'll discuss that in the next chapter. For the sake of a basic introduction to the concept I will concentrate solely on e-books in this chapter.

How to get started:

Simply post a gig saying *you will review any e-book seller submits to you* (if there certain types of books you don't care to deal with you should make that known upfront erotica/gay/etc)

As with all your sale description videos, be sure to include a friendly and engaging video featuring yourself describing what it is you are offering what you will do - including video in your sale description has been proven to be a big selling point for buyers because they want to know they're dealing with.

How to set yourself apart from other sellers

Want to know the secret for getting more sales? Offer more for the money- simple as that.

When everybody else is selling 1 review for five dollars, **you should be to selling 2 or even 3 for the same price.**

Most review buyers are e-book authors with multiple titles and often times they have a limited promotional budgets to work with. So an offer like this represents an *outstanding value* that is just too good to pass up!

Have your buyers to provide their own reviews - this serves a dual purpose and provides an advantage for you as a seller.

1. The buyer will provide *exactly* what they want in their review. It's hard to be upset with a review that you submit for yourself right?

2. By asking the buyer to provide their own review you no longer have to invest valuable time reading books and coming up with your own synopsis. It becomes nothing more than a *cut-and-paste* affair that takes a few minutes at best.

#5 Physical Product Reviews

As I alluded to in the last chapter there's also reviews that can be done for *physical products* as well in places such as Amazon.com and more. Sellers of products in these places counts on building up a collection of positive reviews to *prime the pump* for future sales. You can help them out by offering your services as a physical product reviewer.

The process of leaving a review on physical products is generally the same as with e-books however logistically it can be a little bit more complex. For example Amazon allows buyers to leave two different classes of reviews, *verified* and *unverified* with unverified reviews carrying far less weight and depending upon how Amazon feels, it may not even show up on the sale page at all!

The general way to be a *verified status* is to make a purchase through Amazon which defeats the purpose of making a profit on fiverr therefore it would seem an impossible task.

The loophole
Buyers who are keen on getting reviews for their products have one option in this situation; give out free *gift certificates*.

If the buyer would like you to be a verified purchaser and leave a review for them they can provide you with a *gift certificate code* which you can receive via email for an Amazon purchase. Once you redeem your code Amazon will pack and ship your product to you and you can leave your review with all of the credibility bestowed upon a verified purchaser.

Think about what I just said. Effectively you're getting paid five dollars for your review *and* in addition that you're getting tons of free stuff as well - not a bad position to be in is it?!

How to get started:

Putting up a simple listing on Fiverr (Be sure to include video) and letting sellers know you will do *verified product reviews* for them will generally jumpstart things. You must be sure to let buyers know that they need to provide you with a gift code so that you can purchase as a *verified buyer* (no other way has as much impact) and that's basically all there is to it.

You should be aware of the fact that many buyers will need to be educated a little bit about the process so your description should explain very clearly the steps that are necessary for them to get their review done in the shortest period of time and make things go smoothly.

You should also set your expected time to complete out 4 to 5 days to allow for shipping etc. so that you are not penalized by fiverr for taking too long.

How to set yourself apart from other sellers

The key here is to write great reviews and make sure you offer higher value than any other reviewer in this category.

Don't lose touch with your buyer because if they have one product it's likely they have many others which will lead to additional reviews and more free items pouring in on a regular basis.

It should be noted however, you're not going to find as many buyers for this type of sale as you would an e-book simply because of all the steps it takes to make it happen. That being said, you do still get the advantages of a lot of free stuff if you do it right!

#6 Do Silly PR Stuff

.

Although there is a lot of professional business conducted each day on fiverr there's also many sellers there that don't take things all that seriously.

One such seller is **badbeehavior** for $5 he'll dress up like a pirate complete with set design and all and deliver whatever message *ye be like'n*.... Odd? Sure. Popular? Absolutely! He's a top rated seller and consistently featured on the lead page for his category.

Fiverrs Fun & Bizarre category is where you are likely to find anything. The sky is the limit. This opens up some promotional possibilities too. Smart sellers have learned to take their wacky antics and parlay them into big bucks as *promotional stunts* and buyers are responding in droves!

- Got a great body? Dress up in a sexy bikini and deliver a message on cam or hold someone's website address on a card.

- On the other end of the spectrum, are you in *god-awful* shape but have a great sense of humor about it? Refer to the above tip and do the same – it's not pretty but it sells… believe me, people will pay for it…the more over the top you are the better it does.

- Offer prank videos – let your imagination go wild on this one (just keep it legal)

- Voice impersonations. Can you do a great Sean Connery or Morgan Freeman? Turn that skill into cash by selling birthday wish recordings or answering machine messages

- Cartoon voices – I did some quick research and it's surprising how FEW sellers there are in this niche. Work on your best Bugs Bunny or Mickey Mouse impersonation and see what happens.

- Drag out last year's Halloween costume and see if you can find a way to use it in a gig offer.

- Does your dog do stupid tricks on command? Make him earn his keep! Get him on cam and cash in on all those dog lovers on fiverr with businesses to promote.

- Go through your kid's toy box and fish out those funny hand puppets you bought for them years ago and use them to make humorous messages or amusing company promos. Go crazy and add backdrops and even music!

Your income in this segment is ONLY limited by your creativity and willingness to be a little silly for the sake of a darn good payday!

How to get started:

Keep it simple at first. Try a promotional listing with your own personal brand of wacky, weird or strange mixed it. And see what kind of response you get. One of the great parts about fiverr is that you can try your ideas out and have them live on the site in only minutes.

Stick to these tips and you'll come up with your own winners

- Humor sells so keep it light

- Don't' take yourself too seriously. Have fun with what you're doing and it will come across to the buyer.

- Always ask yourself "Would my buyer want this associated with his/her product or service?"

- Be original – fiverr has enough pirate stuff, find your own thing…

How to set yourself apart from other sellers:

- Offer multi scripts for one low price.

- Give buyers a choice of colors, sets or costumes

- Be open to custom work – your buyer may be the best source of your next great gig so don't be too quick to think you have covered all the bases.

#7 Monetize Your Hidden Talents

If outrageous behavior isn't your style you can still make incredible money on fiverr using your own brand of personal talent. Can you sing or play an instrument? Perhaps you're good at magic or you can beat box better than anyone you know. Practically anything has the potential to become top earning gig if you apply the right blend of skill, promotion and enthusiasm to it.

Some of the top producing talent gigs are:

- I will sing your song (provided by the buyer)

- I will record an original piece of music

- I will provide a collection of 25 original royalty free songs for you to use anywhere

- I will translate your document from Spanish/ Italian/ French etc. to English or vice versa

- I will add background music to your song

- I will create your logo in dominos and knock them over

How to get started:

Dig into your personal collection of hobbies and activities and see if anything you enjoy doing can be monetized as a product or service to others. Often times just about anything can. It's simply a matter of *framing the offer* correctly and establishing a benefit to the buyer.

How to set yourself apart from other sellers

If you have a bunch of listings that are going nowhere fast, keep your eyes and ears open to new possibilities. Tastes change and trends pop up literally overnight.

If you want to ride the latest wave of popularity (hopefully all the way to the bank) check out **trends.google.com** this is one of the fastest ways I know of to get your finger on the "*pulse*" of the masses and come up with new sales ideas.

#8 Sell EBooks

Selling your eBooks on fiverr is a no brainer. You won't get the kind of traffic of say an Amazon.com but the profit is much better! It's also a free way to gain additional publicity for yourself or a series.

Top selling writers user fiverr as a way to jump start a series by selling the first copy on fiverr and embedding links to a sale page or email gathering landing page in order to up sell the next books directly. It's pure *marketing 101,* and it works like gangbusters!

If you have some existing books that are collecting dust in your back catalog or hard drive, they could be finding new life on fiverr as well. Again, listing costs you *nothing* so why not give it a try?

Even if you are not an author you can still play the eBook game. Spend some time researching the *public domain* books and you'll come up with hundreds, if not thousands of very marketable books that simply need to be reformatted and perhaps visually updated a bit*. It's all free, and perfectly legal too, thanks to the U.S. Copyright laws – Thank you Uncle Sam!

If you really want to be cheeky about it you can go right back to fiverr and hire all that done too!

How to get started:

If you are an existing author then dig into your personal catalog and pull out some gold. Get it up on fiverr and that's all there is to it. If your book was a good seller before it's likely to find new life again on fiverr.

Public domain books are almost as easy. Anything published before 1923 is up for grabs – seriously. All you need to do is get a copy of whatever you think will appeal to the buying masses, get it into a word processor and format it for either PDF or DOC format, maybe add some pictures or put in some new content.

Really, the choice is up to you. Once you get it done, write your sale description –put up a promo video and then - BOOM! You my friend are published author!

How to set yourself apart from other sellers:

There are a plethora of ways to pull in buyers on fiverr and set yourself apart. I know I've said this before, but again this advice holds true: *Always give more for the money than your competition does.* In this instance why not give away three or four additional public domain books from the same topic with the purchase of the first one? Talk about value!

While I'm tossing out ideas here, let me give you another good one. Why not embed your website domain within each book? That way your new reader may be inclined to visit your website or blog as well.

You could even go further and point them towards a landing page that collects their email so that when you have new things to offer you have them on a mailing list pre-loaded and ready to go!

#9 Guest Blog

The failure rate for blogs is phenomenal and this is due to one thing above all else; It's difficult to run a blog 365 days of the year. Most beginning bloggers vastly underestimate the amount of time and the multitude of skills it takes to operate a truly world-class blog.

The truth is; if you want to be successful with a blog it will likely take over your life and every moment of your free time will be invested in it. Especially if you try to do it on your own. This is why successful bloggers learn very early on to *subcontract* out a portion of the work. But it's not always as easy as making the decision to give the work to someone else as you will soon see.

When you think about it, Five bucks is a small price to pay for a little outside help from time to time. I can tell you though from firsthand experience it's not easy to find quality help to fill in when you're not at the helm though.

You have no doubt read endless books and online articles telling you to *just throw the work to a virtual assistant and then go sit on the beach while they do all the heavy lifting.* Blog owners who buy into this line of garbage are in for a serious disappointment (some of you have maybe already found this out the hard way).

The vast majority of online assistants are based in the Philippines. I am American, however, I live in the Philippines. I have firsthand knowledge of the people here and I can tell you that although they are very sweet people, the vast majority of them are *not* up to the task of filling in for a standard American or European owned blog.

And I'm not telling you all this to break on Filipinos or their culture. I'm telling you this because I'm painting a picture of how open the market *truly is* for quality bloggers who can competently speak English, form a sentence and express an idea in depth. I can tell you firsthand, the work is there if you want it. All you have to do is reach out and claim your share of it. You will never run out of work if you want it.

By the way, you don't need fiverr to make this work - Find some blogs with a large subscriber base in an area you may be interested in or have knowledge of and write the owners. Ask them if they're open to paying for a little outside help. You might be able to strike a bargain and ease the owner's workload at the same time.

How to get started:

All you need is a word processing program. Microsoft Word is considered the industry standard however, if you can't swing the cash it takes for *Word* you can pick up a program called openoffice.org it's absolutely free and totally up to the task. Once you get everything installed you're in business.

Take some time to search around fiverr and see what other bloggers are offering. A quick search and the time of writing this book revealed most bloggers are working at a rate of 300 to 500 words for five dollars.

Early on I would suggest you offer a higher basic word count - say 600 to 700 words at least until your feedback builds to a level where people begin to recognize you and the quality work you are putting out. At that point you could lower your word count or even just completely separate yourself from fiverr altogether and go direct with a few key clients *

considering that fiverr takes 20% of your earnings that's probably not such a bad idea anyway!

How to set yourself apart from other sellers:

There's no substitute here for personal experience and the ability to string together words in a coherent fashion.

Stick to what you know or what you can easily research and you need go no further. If you have a certain niche that you would like to concentrate on then let it be known in your sale description. People will seek you out.

As I said before there's plenty of work out there, all you need to do is let people know that you are available to do it and you will never – *ever* run out of work!

#10 Edit Or Proof Read

If you have an English literary degree collecting mountains of dust or experience in copyediting you'll find a very welcome home on fiverr because we need you!

Most authors come from a wide variety of backgrounds and very few have literary or English degrees (myself included). That being said, most authors have no problem getting their ideas down on paper but they may have failed to use the proper punctuation or inadvertently created a run-on sentence or two. This is where your parent's investment in your four-year college English lit degree may finally start to pay for itself! *

In fact I know of one college English major currently earning spectacular money on fiverr right from her dorm room editing he books in her spare time!

How to get started:

There's no accessories needed for this one. Simply post your gig and let people know that you will review their books or documents and check for grammatical and punctual mistakes.

How to set yourself apart from other sellers:

Take a look round fiverr and see what the current crop of editors and readers are offering and see if you can *one up* them by offering a faster or more in-depth service.

This is another one of those gigs that can lead to a lot of repeat business so be sure to collect your clients names and emails and keep your name in front of them on a semiannual basis so that they don't forget about you when their next job comes around.

#11 Critique Others

Sometimes people are just a little too close to their own projects and the need an outside opinion. This is really one of those gigs that doesn't cost anything and it's pretty easy to do. Everybody has an opinion (oftentimes you'll hear it even when you don't want to!) So why not get paid for it?

There's a lot of different ways you can approach this gig but the most popular is website evaluation. People spend a lot of time and effort developing their site and it's important to know how the end user will interact with it. Therefore critiquing can be a valuable asset to the web developer.

How to get started:

Post a gig saying you will evaluate your buyer's website. Let them know in great detail what you will be doing, for example here's how I would approach this:

I will evaluate your website for you and give you my thoughts on its strong and weak points. I will evaluate all your links to make sure that they are going where they need to and I will let you know if your site is loading correctly *

*You can find all kinds of free websites that give statistics on website performance that you can give to your buyer that will boost credibility such as link performance and loading time statistics.

If you have some working knowledge of website seo you may wish to take things a step further and offer helpful tips on how to optimize your client's site for better performance as part of the deal (or an upsell)

How to set yourself apart from other sellers:

This is a very individualistic service and no two are ever alike. The sellers who will win the lion's share of clients are the ones who offer *the largest amount of services in the fastest time*.

#12 SEO

If you spend any amount of time doing business online at all eventually the subject of Google and search engines in general will come up. Google's presence in modern-day business is so pervasive that it has spawned whole industry segments that are dedicated to figuring out how to interact with it. One of these industries is known as search engine optimization (SEO for short).

In a nutshell, SEO is the practice of selecting keywords and optimizing your websites content in such a way with them that users searching for said key word will hopefully be able to locate you though being featured on the top page search results… confused? You should be!

Businesses spend thousands of dollars each year trying to optimize your website for a whole host of keywords in order to gain top rankings within Google, Bing and others. It's a never-ending race to stay on top and few people understand how to do it properly. This presents yet again another gold mine of opportunity for those who are *in the know*.

A deeper explanation of search engine optimization is called for here but it's beyond the scope of this simple book. Suffice it to say if you understand how to optimize a website or how to properly promote it to the search engines you can make some great money.

If you don't understand the deeper mechanics of search engine optimization you can still get in on the gold rush. All you need is some proper software that will do the job for you I highly suggest Blast-O-Matic.com it's an android-based program that works on your cell phone or tablet.

With Blast-O-Matic all you need to do is enter your client's website address and press *go*. It will then "blast" your client's website out to as many as 15,000+ search engines all over the world and in turn gain your client some much needed back links that will aid in driving increases of traffic to his door.

How to get started:

There are several different ways to approach SEO services:

- you could write keyword rich blog articles for insertion in your clients site

- you could offer *keyword density reports* spelling out where they could improve their sites performance by outlining what words are working and which ones are not.

- You could offer to use your large social media list to promote their site

- or you could use software such as Blast-O-Matic.com

These are only for a few possible scenarios. SEO is a multimillion dollar industry that is like a monster that just cannot be fed. There's always work to do and there's always new clients coming on board who are clueless and looking for help.

Personally I have made several thousand dollars on fiverr and many of my clients have since that time moved over into larger *contracted positions* with me. Some of them are happily paying as much as five figures a year for my services.

This is the power of a well put together Fiverr plan!

How to set yourself apart from other sellers:

Clients in this niche want to be made to feel like you are on their side and that you understand their needs. Many fiverr sellers are only after the quick *turn and burn* and this is a huge mistake. These sellers fail to understand that SEO is a nonstop process. You can't just do it once and be done. It's a continuous thing. By adopting the short term strategy they are leaving thousands of dollars a year on the table.

If you can teach your clients that SEO must be a part of their *yearly ongoing budget*, not just a one-time expense, you will be setting yourself up for ever higher amounts of return work. I have clients that have been with me for over 5 years, all because I took the time to explain to them early on how to implement a proper SEO strategy.

Not everyone listens to my advice of course, but I have little doubt that those who do will be with me for years to come.

#13 Build A Website For Your Buyer

.Not all that long ago most businesses may or may not have had a website. These days telling people you don't have a website would be like saying you have a business without a phone. You just don't do it! Even though we all understand that this is a fact these days, few of us still have the technical know-how to pull it off for ourselves. This is another situation where a little bit of knowledge can lead to an awful lot of financial gain.

Most of us lead lives that are far too busy to sit down and learn a new skill such as website design, or at least that's what many people think to be true. A few years ago website design was a bit of a *dark art* but that was before WordPress.

WordPress makes it easy to create quality looking websites even if you know very little about computers in general. In just a few days of playing around with the software can gain enough information to put together websites for other people (who won't take the time for themselves) and literally *learn while you earn*!

How to get started:

Create a couple of sample websites to display in your listings that will show the quality of your work and give your potential buyer something visualize before he makes a purchase.

Be sure to offer lots of upsell options (gig extras) there are literally millions of things you can do here to wring out extra money. The key is to offer the initial service and a fantastic price and get your buyer in the door, after that then it's just a matter of determining your client's budget and shaping your additional offers accordingly.

Advanced tip:

If you have the technical know-how invest the time to learn a new skill, I would suggest you talk to a company such as hostgator.com and learn about their *reseller packages*. This could set you up as a one stop shop for all your clients website needs.

How to set yourself apart from other sellers:

Success in this niche is all about offering *options* and *packages* that your clients find appealing at *prices* that are hard to pass up. There are so many people packed into this industry that everyone starts to look a little bit the same and there's not much uniqueness to be found amongst the group.

Because you're dealing with an *intangible product* it's easy to give a little on price. All you really dealing with is a time-based commodity. So figure out what kind time you have into a project and price your work accordingly on all of your basic offers and gig extras.

#14 Sell Premade Sites

Another great tactic that works even better times is to set up the reseller hosting I mentioned earlier with a company such as hostgator.com And sell off premade "turn key" one or two page mini sites… there are still LOTS of potential for upsells here too so it doesn't just stop at five bucks!

How to get started:

1. set up a reseller account

2. create a website with its own unique domain from within your master hosting account

3. develop the site using WordPress. Make it generic so that pictures and text can easily be changed

4. list your new site for sale on fiverr for the basic price of $5 (you could make it include a year of free hosting as well which would be an outrageously good deal no matter how you look at it)

5. construct your gig extras to be had on bills and whistles such as social media plug-ins, photo galleries, or any other number of things that can be easily added to basic WordPress sites with just a few clicks

How to set yourself apart from other sellers:

As far as I'm aware as of the writing of this book there is nobody currently doing this on fiverr.

#15 Sell Brandable Reports

As I talked about earlier on this book, owning a blog or website is time intensive. Faced with a lack of time, it's not always easy for blog owners to come up with fresh content. Why not sell a collection of articles for buyers to use on their own websites or blogs?

Some sellers prefer to sell packs of articles with their own website or blog listed on the bottom with the understanding that these articles can be freely distributed by anyone who has them, however, their website must not be removed from the article. I'm here to tell you right now, that's never going to happen in a million years!

Better to just sell the articles as nameless reports and let buyers put whoever's name they choose on them. As long as you capture the buyers email address. You will always have them in the sales funnel to sell them more later on.

Continuing with the brandable theme, why not create a brandable e-book, (Sometimes referred to as a *private label*), and allow other fiverr users to sell it? You can build the subject matter around things you can link to your personal affiliates and reap the benefits of someone else's distribution efforts. This can be a true win-win situation for both of you.

How to get started:

All you need for this one is word processing software and an opinion to write from. While I can't help you with the opinion, you have to do that part on your own, I can point you to a really good word processing package that's free of charge at OpenOffice.org

How to set yourself apart from other sellers:

Concentrate on one of the more popular niches such as

- diet
- weight loss
- exercise
- making money
- family budgets
- investments
- website development
- search engine optimization
- government or political issues
- social causes

These are only a few of many constantly popular topics and never go out of vogue. Put together a collection of 20 to 25 articles of 500 to 600 words or so centered around any one of these topics and you'll have enough to get started.

#16 Design Ebook Covers

Every successful book author understands one thing. No matter how good the content is buyers will never get close enough to see it unless the cover grab their attention first.

Amazon.com recently reported that as many as 5000 new Kindle e-books are being posted every single day on their site. That represents an astounding number of potential clients, all in need of a cover that will attract new potential reader's attention. With this kind of competition clearly average work just isn't going to cut it.

Take a look at the example below. It was created with specially designed software made specifically for creating e-book covers.

At first glance it looks like a real book. Actually it's not. It's a photorealistic 3-D rendering sitting on top of a real picture of rope. If you're not looking at it very carefully you can't really be sure that it doesn't exist in real life.

It's this type of quality that sells your service to the client. It would be a mistake to believe you could compete using the free software that comes with your computer. If you want to make money designing e-book covers you need to have the very best software available.

How to get started:

Go here to pick up a copy of 360 Ebook Maker
http://bit.do/3D-bookmaker

How to set yourself apart from other sellers:

Spend some time playing with the software. Create a huge portfolio for your buyers and post as many pictures as you can on fiverr to show that and work your capable of.

The beauty of this software is how fast you can change angles & create all new perspectives. This makes it possible to offer two, three, four or more different angles or even backgrounds to your customer for little to no additional work at all for just $5!

#17 Compose A Jingle

If you're the creative music type you can put your skills to could use composing quick 30 second jingles. These are not so common on Internet sites but they are quite popular in applications such as radio and TV commercials.

Writing advertising jingles is a bit of a dying art so there's not much competition for it but the demand is still strong. Composing jingles doesn't take an awful lot of skill and oftentimes you don't even have to set anything to music.

If you compose your gig right you can simply sell *just the lyrics* and save yourself an awful lot of work….and then possibly offer the music to go with your new lyrics as a gig extra.

How to get started:

Just posted gig on fiverr like this: "*I will create lyrics for your product or services advertising jingle*" or something to that effect

once you made a sale then conduct a small interview with your buyer to find out:

- what his product or service is

- the top three or so highlights your buyer considers most important (you'll need these for lyric ideas)

- determine where your buyers price fits in the pricing spectrum is a high-end or the best bargain on the market? That might be a key to the direction your lyrics take.

If you want to make really quick work out of this part of the job simply ask your buyer this; "tell me about your product" - your buyer will instantly give you his opinion on what the most important aspects of his product are!

Simply using his or her own words for direction is the best way you can go because basically you're just laying out *their thoughts* in musical form. Psychologists will tell you there is nothing more pleasing to the human mind than the sound of one's own words!

How to set yourself apart from other sellers:

This gig is all about *service*. In order to make your buyer happy, you need to be fast, friendly and display a good amount of talent as well as professionalism in delivery.

If you want to put the best professional spin on things, why not provide the lyrics on a letterhead via PDF - with something such as *(your company name) Professional Music services* On top?

This will brand you as a *professional* in the eyes of your buyer. And if you do things right, you'll be smart enough to include an email on your letterhead as well, so that you can be contacted *directly* next time your buyer has a job to do.

#18 Create Cartoons

This is a pretty wide open segment and it can be approached in several different ways – all of them are hugely profitable. Here is my top 3 "*Best of the best*".

- **Draw Client Caricatures** – Have your client email you a copy of himself and apply your special style to it.

- **Illustrate A Concept** – I kick out tons of books each year. When I need to have an illustration I choose to use a vectorized drawing rather than a photo. It's neater and cleaner plus the colors "pop" more.

- **Sell Cartoon Packs** – Recently I've noticed a trend developing. An artist will draw a caricature in 10 or so "poses" and sell them as a set. This is a brilliant idea because from a buyer's standpoint the product becomes infinitely more usable. It also assures return business should they ever need additional poses or modified artwork.

-

 How to get started:

Bust out your favorite illustration program and get to scribbling. Sketch out a portfolio of your own and include at least 10 to 12 examples of your work in your listing.

What if you can't draw a straight line to save your life? That's still no excuse to overlook this profitable segment. There are a plethora of sites around the web dedicated to serving your creative needs.

Go to different sites such as *99designs.com* , *Odesk.com* or any of the other thousands of subcontractor sites to be found around the web and commission a "package" of unique drawings to be done *exclusively* for you.

Once your artist submits the final product to you, repackage them and post them up on fiverr.

The beauty of this system is you only have to do the work once and then you can sell these designs over and over again - possibly even for years!

The key to making this work is to be sure they are as *generic*, yet *appealing* as possible so they can be used in many different applications - by many different buyers.

How to set yourself apart from other sellers:

Variety-as they say "*is the spice of life*", it's also how you make more money on fiverr! You need to fill your listings with a wide array of diverse ideas. Don't limit your opportunities here by stickking to just one segment or topic.

Spend a little time finding out what sells. There simply is no replacement for good research. Presentation is *also* important in the final products too. And above all else make sure that you write a quality description being sure to cover any questions your buyer may have.

Demonstrate how flexible your designs are by showing your designs in use and giving your buyers a few additional *use ideas* to jumpstart their imagination.

One of the best bits of advice I ever received as a salesman was from an old advertising executive who told me "*Most times buyers don't even know they have a need for your product until you teach them!*" Think about this next time you're laying out a sale description or writing a bit of ad copy.

#19 Video Blog Review

Youtube is the world's 2nd largest search engine. That being said, it's also one heck of a lot easier to get noticed on than its big brother, google! Smart advertisers know that they need to have their products on YouTube but not all of them have the time to orchestrate the entire process. That's where you come in.

There are so many good ideas you could incorporate Youtube into that all of them put together could make a book unto themselves! Here's the top producing Youtube related gig that successful fiverrs have shared with me:

Review based video blogging is hot. And by the way, it's not just exclusively limited to YouTube either. Most people don't even realize that you can actually embedded video in your Amazon reviews as well. This is still a fledgling program and as of this writing I've only seen two examples so offering this as an alternative could put you in a field of your own for quite some time

People respond *MASSIVELY* to video as compared to simple text. So sell your services as a video reviewer. If you already have a large YouTube following, you can monetize it in all new ways with this method.

Even if you *don't* have a following, smart buyers will still find value in your services because the more voices speaking positively about the product that are out there, the better they will be perceived by the general public.

How to get started:

If you don't already have a YouTube account (known in their lingo as a *channel*) take a few minutes and get one set up. There's no cost to do so, and it only takes about 15 minutes.

The good news is; there's no need to go all "Hollywood" in order to pull this off. Just keep your equipment setup simple and let your personality shine through and you'll do just fine. In fact being a little "raw" and unstaged may actually have its advantages when it comes to credibility.

You don't need anything more than an adequately lit environment and a desktop PC cam with a decent mic so people can understand what you're saying. From there, just let it rip!

How to set yourself apart from other sellers:

The old *two-for-one* or even *three for one* offer is a great way to provide exceptional value and jumpstart a stampede of buyers.

Once you've built up a reputation as a quality reviewer and gained some decent feedback scores, you can trim things back to one video review per five dollar sale if you so choose.

One more idea… *and it's a GOOD ONE:*

There's no need to give away the whole farm for five dollars. You could use this idea as a *premium gig extra* as well. For example: Sell a basic product or e-book review for $5 as you normally would and then offer a *video bonus* upgrade for $20-$25 more!

As of this writing there is absolutely NOBODY doing this on fiverr – What the heck are you waiting for?

Go, man go! Get that listing posted on fiverr RIGHT NOW!

#20 Sell A Physical Product

Did you know fiver has a category for physical products? Yep, it's true!

Granted margins are tight when your net profit is only slightly over $4 in most cases. However, if you are in a position to create something physical that still leaves money on the table after all is said and done then you will find yourself amongst a very select group of fiverr sellers (and surrounded by very little competition).

I met a fiverr member that sold tiny little handmade finger puppets imported from Columbia for just a few cents each that made over 7000 sales marketing them as children's story time play sets.

Another seller I know of made small origami animals and sent them via mail

A member of my own staff does beautiful calligraphy writing and sells her services to wedding planners and never wants for ready buyers (especially around spring time).

How to get started:

Do a few samples of your work, take pictures if its relevant and write a detailed description of what your buyers can expect to receive (and when).

If possible why not include a video of you making your product as you describe it? I *guarantee* buyers will respond and will likely be fascinated to see a demonstration of your skill in action.

Think about how many infomercials you've sat through in a lifetime… *come on*… you know I'm right! …we're all guilty of this at least once in our lives!

How to set yourself apart from other sellers:

This is an easy one. The key here is to just do your own thing. This is a category on fiverr where it truly pays to be unique.

Think about it this way; you're asking a buyer to purchase a product that they will have to wait for so it better be special and it most certainly had better be worth the wait!

#21 Beta Test

In house product testing is big business, Car companies do it, food companies do it and the software industry is certainly no stranger to it either. However, within the last decade or so there has been a shift in the way many companies "shake out the junk" in their new releases, one of the top ways they do this is through *Beta testing*.

Beta testing can be accomplished in a few different ways. Gaming software companies hand out limited free copies of new releases to key reviewers who in turn trade their opinions for cash or inside bargains.

Car companies don't even go that far these days as they simply release the final product up front. If nobody dies (or an acceptable number do) the product is deemed "good enough"*

Beta testing (although seemingly free), still comes at a huge cost to companies of all sizes due to product development and initial sampling costs. With that being said, many smaller time companies have resorted to *micro job sites* such as fiverr to lower their testing expenses.

* I wish I were joking about that but I'm not. I come from the auto industry. I've witnessed this behavior first hand many times. Remember the Toyota Prius brake failure scandal, The Ford Pinto exploding gas tanks or their Explorer rollover debacle? I rest my case!

Finding your niche in the Beta testing industry

Beta testing basically falls into two major categories; *hardware* and *software*. While it may be conceivable to find a few hardware manufacturers on fiver that are looking for testers it's not likely that you'll find a constant supply of them. Software on the other hand is a whole different deal.

Within the software side of things you also have additional sub-segments as well such as

- apps
- websites
- and of course, externally provided software itself.

There's really no need to limit yourself to anyone in particular subset.

How to get started:

Post a gig on fiverr letting buyers know that you will test and evaluate their product, app, website or software. For the basic $5 fee

Always make it clear upfront that if there's any cost involved in securing a copy of what they want evaluated that it is the buyer's responsibility to provide the funds to make the purchase.

By the way you may be contacted by people selling *physical products* on Amazon as well - as I mentioned elsewhere in this book, just be sure they provide you with a gift card if you need to make a purchase in order to complete your review.

In most cases though all that's called for here is a little bit of your time to play with whatever is provided to you from your buyer and your opinion of the experience you had with it.

Once you've made your evaluation, knockdown three or 400 words and send it off to your buyer and that is pretty much all there is to it.

How to set yourself apart from other sellers:

Building your status up to become a top-level reviewer involves being available to *everyone*, in *every way* to review *everything.* Don't turn a job down – *ever*.

9 times out of 10 buyers looking to have a product reviewed will likely have *additional products* waiting in the wings. So every one job you accomplish could conceivably open the door to many hidden opportunities and turn into some potentially consistent direct work.

#22 Debug

The next logical progression after beta testing is of course fixing any problems that have been discovered. If you have software development skills then putting yourself out there as a beta tester is a great marketing move for you to make because it can open the doors to further higher-paying work, such as fixing the problem!

I've met far more than one formerly starry eyed entrepreneur who has been stuck with a half completed software program after subcontracting its creation out to one of the four corners of the earth.

Software developers, especially in foreign countries are a notoriously flaky bunch. Prices change, personal problems arise, excuses come in just about every form you can possibly imagine and eventually, at some point, communication inevitably breaks down. The end result is a very dissatisfied and disillusioned group of people looking for someone to bail them out of their misery.

Applying your coding skills here (along with some understanding and tender mercy) can net you some *huge returns.*

How to get started:

$5 is not enough of a wage to take on any type of software related problem, so you have to approach this gig with a little creatively. Post a sale on fiverr letting buyers know that you will *evaluate* their unfinished, app, website or software and deliver "plan of action". This serves three purposes:

1. it does not continue getting in over your head without seeing everything the work entails.

2. It makes you five bucks just for having a look "*under the hood*" and giving your opinion.

3. And set you up for a much bigger payday when the *real work* begins

Once your buyer makes a purchase then have them send you a copy of the software or website in question and any relevant passcodes you'll need.

Once you've gotten done tinkering with it to see if anything can be done, write up a quick PDF proposal along with a quote for an hourly or set price and be absolutely sure that you remember to include your direct email and maybe even your phone number on the top of the quote. This will allow your buyer to contact you directly to work with you one-on-one.

How to set yourself apart from other sellers:

Never take on a job unless you are sure you do the work.

And above all else remember: Your buyer has already been burned once, you *must absolutely* make him feel like that will not happen again! When you make a promise - be damn sure to deliver on it.

'Nuff said.

#23 Be An Authority

People will pay for your advice. You could offer advice or critiques on all kinds of things from website designs, business plans or even relationship advice. You would be surprised how open people are to the opinions of a stranger. The key to adding value to your opinions is to establish yourself as an *authority figure*.

The fastest way to become an authority is to just start talking and blogging. Join several forums within your niche and promote your site via your signature line as you participate in related discussions. The more you do it, the more recognized become. It's sort of a self-fulfilling thing.

A word of warning here: be careful to always read and understand your forums rules concerning self-promotion. Some take a dim view of blatant self-promotion while others could care less. Be sure you understand what's permitted and what isn't so that you don't annoy the forum moderators and end up getting banned.

It's a good idea to lurk around for a little while and see how other users are posting and how other site members react to each other before trying anything on your own.

Slow and steady wins the race. Build your reputation as an authority by posting sincere, helpful and useful comments. Don't be in a hurry to plaster the entire Internet with back links to your gigs either. The links will come on their own. All you need to do is come up with useful and relevant answers to the issues being addressed within the forum.

If other members find value in what you have to say, they will automatically give you credit you deserve and respond by wanting to know more about you and your gigs links or website without being asked to do so.

How to get started:

If you haven't already done so start a WordPress.com website or join blogger.com both sites are free and will allow you a great platform to begin broadcasting your own unique point of view to the world (the first step in establishing yourself as an authority figure).

Be sure to set a schedule for regular posts and stick to it. Establishing yourself as a next takes time. The best way to approach this is to map out 20 or 30 topics to write on and pick one each day or week and knock out a quick 500 to 600 words. Before you know it shall have a body of work you can refer others to that will easily establish you as somebody who has something important to say.

The next step is to parlay your new authority status into a fiverr income. While fiverr doesn't approve of links to the outside world you can still accomplish this by giving a quick link to your blog in your *about me* section. As of this writing that still legal.

Is this gig for you?

When it comes to establishing credibility with the public there are no easy shortcuts. As you have learned above, there is clearly work that needs to be done to lay the groundwork before you can reap the benefits - and it takes time. If you're looking for a fast buck on fiverr this is probably not the gig for you.

With that being said, if you are already actively running a blog this can be a nice way to additionally monetize all the hard work that you put in so far. It's also a way to pick up some new subscribers!

#24 Be A Geek

Just because most of the modern world spends it's time in front of a keyboard that does not mean we all understand what's going on…. This is where a little specialized knowledge can go a long, long way…

I remember years ago when I heard that you can make money hooking people's VCRs up. "You've got to be kidding me" I thought. "People really pay for that?" Oh yes they do…by the *THOUSANDS*! In fact, I earned my way through college installing car stereos. Mind you, this was back in the day when it only required two screws and about five wires to do the job - *15 minutes tops.* Yet people would dole out as much as $30 or $40 bucks for me to do the job for them, simply because there was a *knowledge gap**

*I would often times hear people tell me that they were afraid they were going to burn their car to the ground in an electrical fire if they did something wrong so it gave them peace of mind tiring professional to do the work for them - fine by me, Cha-Ching!

When people don't have answers *they are willing to pay for them.* You can set yourself up for a nonstop supply of sales if you can be the one to provide the right answers

Serve as computer I.T. support

If you work in one of the various segments of the computer industry want to turn your knowledge and do some after-hours cash by answering questions? My best friend serves as an IT for a large American publishing company. He sits in his office all day and manages a network of over 25,000 computers countrywide. It never occurred to him that he could have posted IT related assistance on fiverr but in reality is one of the strongest segments on the site.

IT support is a great gig because many small companies cannot afford to keep somebody on staff and sometimes all they want is one or two questions unanswered, it's not worth having someone on the payroll when you don't need them all the time. You can fill that role for them by offering your services.

Answer questions etc.

The same thing applies here as it does above. Posting a simple gig saying "I will answer your IT related question" will see you hit with a wide variety of questions from confused buyers who just need a little guidance. Its easy money if you know what you're doing and can supply a friendly helping hand to confused buyer.

How to get started:

Think about what specialty skills you possess (*it doesn't even have to be computer-related*) and don't fool yourself into believing that everybody should already know what you know because as you just learned, that's simply not the case!

Maybe you'd like to *add* to your knowledge base or *become* an expert on something. That's easier than you think. Famed marketing guru Dan Kennedy is famous for saying that *in order to be an expert on any subject all you really need to do is read the top three books on that subject and then you will know more than 95% of the public.* That's actually pretty brilliant advice and you should take it into consideration when offering your skills as an "expert" on any subject.

How to set yourself apart from other sellers:

Don't try to be all things to all people with this gig. Stick to the *core subject(s)* that are within your wheelhouse. I say this because when you offer advice on things you're enthusiastic about you'll put more passion and care into delivering a service to your buyer and it will show in the final product.

#25 Retouch Photos

If you're skilled in Photoshop or other similar photo manipulation software you can make some really great money on fiverr. I won't belabor this chapter because I believe most of us know by now what Photoshop is and what it's capable of doing. However, very few people possess the skills to actually use the software to its fullest potential*but if you're one of them you can cash in big time.

Of those that would dare to take a stab at learning, one look by them at the instruction manual for Photoshop will generally send most would-be users running off into the night screaming in horror -have you seen the size of that thing? that looks at the New York phone book! Who's got that kind of time?

Because of Photoshop's versatility there are so many possibilities. The staff at www.FiverrPowerTips.Com polled the top producing graphic artists on fiverr and asked them what works best. Here is what they came up with:

- *photo morphing* - this is basically technique where you take one picture and blended with another stretch or distorted into something completely different

- *photo collages* -the biggest use of this technique is in headers blogs, websites, YouTube channels and Facebook pages.

- *knocking out backgrounds* - customers provide their favorite choice of picture and the artist/seller will remove backgrounds replacing it with one that is pure white or see-through.

- ***retouching*** - pretty standard stuff. Things like removing red eyes blotches and blemishes

- ***custom 15 minute work*** - this is a rising trend and one that is designed to catch jobs that perhaps may have been missed. Limiting the work to 15 minutes allows sellers to upsell additional time through gig extras (thereby scoring larger payouts in the process!)

How to get started:

All you really need to do is post 10 or so examples of your best work on your sale page along with a few suggestions of the type of work you are capable of and the buyers will find you all on their own.

How to set yourself apart from other sellers:

This gig is about *pure skill.* If you're good you're going to stand out- *and cash in!*

#26 Facebook Company Or Fan Pages

Remember a few chapters back when I mentioned that people used to pay to have their VCRs set up? Again, here's another one of those instances. Not everyone can (or wants to) spend valuable time to set up a Facebook page. Many would prefer to have someone else do it for them… *if the price is right.*

Businesses are constantly under advisement to join the "Facebook revolution". In truth most don't even have a clue *why* they are doing it! But that's perhaps a favorite topic of mine for another time altogether.

With everything else there is to do to run a business in the modern age, adding the time it takes to go through *the Facebook learning curve* just doesn't make sense for most folks, so naturally hiring someone to do the dirty work just makes good financial sense. Especially when the price starts at only five bucks!

How to get started:

If you're already versed in Facebook then you are already ahead of learning curve compared to most people. Why not put up a simple gig offering to create a Facebook fan page or start an account and install pictures? It may seem ridiculously easy to you but for many other people it's like mastering advanced calculus! Knowledge is indeed power!

Once you get your basic listing up you can offer gig extras such as ongoing account maintenance (which in actual practice doesn't really amount to *all that much* but many people believe it does) or you could offer graphics services or multi account set ups for small businesses.

How to set yourself apart from other sellers

Create a few *dummy accounts* and really trick them out with high-end graphics and all the bells and whistles you can throw at them. These will serve as your portfolio examples for perspective buyers.

The key here is to tout your accessibility and flexibility. Buyers want to believe that you are there to help them so make that crystal-clear. You are solving a problem for your buyer and acting as an authority figure so every move you make should reflect that.

#27 Develop Resumes

This is an easy one… there is never a shortage of folks who need to update their resume and frankly there are few things on this earth less exciting to spend your time doing. That puts you in a great spot to …..

Here's a tip: Go get one of the freely available resume creators on the web and plug your client's info into it and "bam!" just like that – you're done. (The beauty of this gig is that few people bother to go looking for a program that will take the drudgery out of the process – so a little knowledge & effort can make you some serious money!)

How to get started:

Post a few examples of your finished work for people to see. Don't have anything yet? That's an easy fix! – The Net is full of examples – simply find one and swap out the info – It doesn't get any easier!

How to set yourself apart from other sellers

Speed sells with this gig. When you pick up a sale it's likely you're dealing with someone who is in need of a job… and soon! Your buyer will deeply appreciate your speed and will likely let others know in your feedback.

#28 Do Press Releases

Some people just are simply no good with words. If you *are* then this is a gig you'll love because it NEVER seems to run out of buyers!

How to get started:

Press releases can make you quick money because they always follow a FORMAT. Who, what, where, when, etc.

Check around to some of the *how to* sites to pick up some tips and then go to work setting yourself up a few templates. Once you make a sale all you'll need to do is fill in the particulars (that your client gives you) and you're off to the races!

How to set yourself apart from other sellers

Offer 2 for 1 deals or better yet, just surprise your buyer and deliver another one FREE…provide service like this and believe me; he or she will be *YOUR* best press release!

#29 Sell Ringtones

Remember the song *SHE BLIDED ME WITH SCIENCE, By Thomas Dolby*? Have you ever wondered what happened to that guy? .I'll tell you – He's busy making a FORTUNE selling ringtones for cell phones! Seriously. If he can do it, so can you!

How to get started:

Download or use one of the many free online ringtone makers and *store you collection where they can be accessed when you need them once you make a sale.

What kind of ringtones sell? In a word – *EVERYTHING* sells – my best advice here is to offer at least 10 ring tones for the basic $5 and always keep an eye on the latest trends.

Above all else, be sure NOT to violate any copyright laws. It's not worth the risk to fight a lawsuit or lose your fiverr account.

*Tip: smart sellers will make their buyers enter an email to access their purchases so that they can hit up their buyers list later for more sales!

How to set yourself apart from other sellers

Sell GIG EXTRAS with huge collections of 20, 30 maybe even 50 to 100 or more – that's how you get the REAL money rolling in!

#30 Do Something Weird

I've seen some strange things indeed during my tenure at FIVERPOWERTIPS.COM, People dressing like furry animals, offering to take a random hit to the groin while holding a buyers message and even one guy playing a musical instruments with his butt (don't ask, I'm *still* trying to get the sight of that one outta my head!)

My point here is that short of doing something that violates Fiverrs TOS, pretty much anything else is open to try. The worst thing that will happen is people may laugh at you… but that may be the point anyway, right?

How to get started:

Get out your camera and get creative. This one's a WIDE OPEN FIELD. I can't tell you what to do here. Only YOU know what you are capable of so don't be afraid to "let it all hang out"….*so to speak*.

How to set yourself apart from other sellers

Try to break new ground. This is not an area where you want to be a "me too" player. Spend some time coming up with your weirdest and wackiest ideas then put it out there and see if you get any response… who knows, *you may go viral!*

#31 Sell Memberships

Do you have a website or subscription based website or circulation? Why not sell memberships to it right on fiverr? Besides the monetary gain the chill enjoy it's kind of a cheeky way to draw free publicity for your product as well. I used to do the same thing on eBay all the time (in fact it still works over there too).

Depending upon what you're selling membership to your site or circulation at $5 may not cover it all. To overcome this you could approach this perceived limitation in several different ways:

- Try selling a one day, one week or one month "trial" - to get your subscribers for them the door.

- Use it as a *loss leader* and then upsell additional products once you've drawn them in.

- Sell just a basic package and then tie in your gig extras as upsells for premium membership upgrades or content.

- Reframe your $5 sale as a "coupon" redeemable towards a larger total sale price.

How to get started:

Let's assume you have a membership website. You could post a gig like this "*I will give you an UNLIMITED access pass to my exclusive site for 7 days*" You would go on to explain what the normal price of membership entails to establish what kind of value you are offering as well as the features and benefits that can be found inside.

If you structured this correctly you would be making mention of the site within the sale page itself. Curious onlookers may feel compelled to go to the site and check it out before committing any kind of money (even if it is only $5)

Long before you post anything on fiverr you should be prepared to harvest every one of your sites visitors in the form of an on-site email collection offer - say perhaps a free e-book or additional information to be sent upon entering your email?

Using this technique is one of the best free ways to drive traffic to your blog or website even if you never make a direct sale from it who cares?! By posting a gig you have created free advertising directly to 20,000,000+fiverr users. Wouldn't you just love to have even 1% of that hitting your website?

How to set yourself apart from other sellers:

Memberships to every possible thing imaginable have been sold for years. There is such a wide variety of possibilities in this arena for membership sale techniques that I've barely scratched the surface of what's possible.

You'll have no problem finding additional ways to apply membership techniques to fiverr if you just spend a little time giving it some deep thought and a small amount of effort.

#32 Provide Professional Services

Done correctly, this gig can be an amazing way to expand your clientele. If you are a professional or accredited expert or serve any form professional community at all, you could offer your services or advice via fiverr*

- bookkeeping
- accounting
- legal
- medical
- astrology
- dieting advice
- relationship advice
- career advice
- life coach

Of course some professions are restricted over state lines by regulations of course use your common sense and check your local laws.

Are you congruent?

I want talk for a minute about *credibility*. If you're going to put yourself out there as a professional and you have to look the part as well as act the part.

If you are offering medical advice then you should be shooting a video preferably in a medical environment (say for example a doctor's office with medical charts in the background) and you should be dressed the part. Doctor's lab coat and all.

If you are offering legal advice it would make sense to shoot your description video in front of a large wall of legal books - the kind that are typically found in any law office library. You should be dressed in professional attire and sitting up straight to project an air of authority.

The same can be said of all the professions listed above as well as any others you may come up with on your own. Don't send your buyer's mixed messages by saying one thing and looking like another. This is known as *congruency* and it is absolutely essential to making top level sales.

How to set yourself apart from other sellers

You can set yourself apart from every other seller by using one word in your sale descriptions "*HELP*" so often sellers choose the wrong words and forget that people are coming to them for help -not to be sold to or have some peddle their latest wares.

When you're selling professional services remembering this can take you a long, long way. Therefore, when you are constructing a gig listing you should always be sure to feature this word to frame yourself as a *compassionate seller* who is there to make the buyer's life less burdensome. For example:

"***For $5 I would LOVE to help you fix your bookwork***" - Have you ever seen a listing like that on fiverr? I seriously doubt you have! Quite a bit different than the average way of putting the hard sell on the buyer isn't it?

Highlighting the word *love*, and coupling it with the word ***help*** frames you as somebody who is not just another *fast buck artist* and *I absolutely guarantee* you're going to get at least an initial look from curious buyers who are in the market for bookkeeping assistance. So be sure to follow up with a great sale description and a killer video to drive your sale home.

#33 Broadcast To Your Social Network

Sites like Facebook & Twitter dominate much of today's marketing discussions. For sellers with large followings on these sites it can represent a potential *goldmine*.

If you have ever taken even the slightest stab at using social media to promote your website or blog and experienced little if anything to show for your efforts, then then deep down in your heart you already know social media is not an easy thing the master.

For most busy people spending hour after hour building followers on twitter and likes on Facebook is a HUGE misuse of time. Far better to pay the five bucks to someone else who already has a following and be done with it… that someone *should be you!*

How to get started:

There are a number of programs, both free and paid they can highly automate the process of social media submission. Here's a few of the best

- **Bufferapp.com** - I use the paid version of this one myself. I started with the free version at first and it proved to be invaluable so I stepped up and things got even better.

- **TweetDeck** - This program is 100% free. It used to incorporate many more features than it currently does however it still serves a purpose and you can't beat the price.

- **HootSuite** - This one is considered the Cadillac of the bunch, so naturally you have to pay for it, and it doesn't come cheap. If all you want to do is promote your fiverr gigs this is probably not the software for you because it's just far too expensive.

A matter which program you choose, I wouldn't suggest you go all in and start tossing cash around in hopes things will work out for you. You can lose a lot of money very quickly if you don't know what you're doing.

I would recommend starting with a free version of *Bufferapp* or *TweetDeck* and feeling your way through the social media jungle first, before getting too crazy with any kind of subscription-based program. Once things began to prove out - then pull the trigger and go big time.

How to set yourself apart from other sellers

I've talked a great deal about social media and many of my books and appearances. I'm consistently disturbed by how little most people understand how to use this vital tool. Let me give you one of my more famous analogies:

Imagine if you will a wine tasting party*. The people in attendance share a common bond (love of wine). The mood is calm and casual and everyone there is generally having a good time discussing their mutual interests.

If this group were on twitter with a would probably gather together under #winetasting

All of a sudden someone kicks open the front door screaming through a bullhorn "***hey everyone, come to*** *my store and buy stuff! It's on sale!*" Can you imagine the look on the crowd's face? It's highly unlikely anyone would be reaching for their wallets. Yet, this silly example has some clear parallels to the way many people approach marketing to the social media crowd.| It's just plain wrong!

Let's rejoin the party in a different scenario. Assume nobody is *crashing the party*, we were *a part of it*. Moving around, interacting with other attendees, sharing stories and *bonding over commonalities*.

If the opportunity presented itself, perhaps you would take out a business card and slip it to a member in attendance as you discuss your shared love of rare French wines and say "*you know, my store just got one of the only cases still left of Chateau Le Pin- if you're interested in taking a look you should stop by this week.*"* …. Smooth…

Chateau Le Pin: At only 500 to 700 cases a year available worldwide at any given time, you're not getting this stuff at Costco!

The point I'm making here is it pays to *be a subtle part of the conversation*, not to loudly hijack it. *Shotgun blasting* your marketing message all over social media is like spinning your tires in the mud, you're doing a lot of work, but you won't get very far.

BONUS

#34 Clone Your Gigs

Think about this for a second and you will see the wisdom in it, especially when you are initially struggling to come up with 20 "*completely original*" gig ideas.

Every fiverr seller can tell you that there are one or two gigs in their offerings that vastly outperform all the others. As for myself I have one that does 4 times the income of all the other 19 combined!

Why not copy your most successful gig and create a 2nd, 3rd or 4th listing? True, you'll have to *spin* them a bit to avoid relisting a straight up copy, but as of this writing fiverr seems to have no problem with this practice!

Cloning your gigs for bigger market share.
Herein lies "*the secret advantage*": Let's assume you have a gig posted offering to design business cards. You post it and then begin burning brain cells looking for other tie in topics (or totally different ones) to add in for your remaining 19 listings. There is a better way to rack up listings and corner the market on business card exposure all at once…

Rather than move on to another segment all together, simply *tweak your listing* just a bit and relist it over and over– like this.

- I will ***design you a killer business card*** for $5

- I will *create a one of a kind business card* for $5

- I will *deliver a professional quality business card design* for $5

Same basic service, but totally different listing! By applying this little known technique you have *radically upped your odds* of being discovered when a buyer goes looking for someone to design a business card (or whatever your niche may be).*

As time goes on you will be able to watch your traffic stats and see which listing is getting the *lion's share* of attention. Meanwhile you could be researching other gigs to try out and perhaps delete your bottom 15 business card gigs and try a new gig posted in 15 different ways.

Wash-rinse-repeat!
Using this process is a terrific way to build up a powerful catalog of gigs. Sure, it will take a little time, but your efforts will be paid back immensely!

Also, **Be sure to use different key words in each listing as this will "spread out the net" a bit wider and offer a larger group of words to be discovered with.*

More Bonus Material:

#35 Supercharge Your Sales With Affiliate Offers

This bonus section is about finding related things to upsell to your existing fiverr buyers email list. (If you haven't already started your buyer list I highly suggest you grab a copy of **33 Fiverr Power Tips** and let me show you how to set it up.)

I'm a big fan of affiliate programs. The beautiful part about them is there is never any upfront investment on your part and there's always something new coming out. Because of this, there is always something you can find to in tie into your latest promotional project.

It's generally a good idea to be a member of several affiliate programs at once. That leaves your options wide open and provides you multiple streams of income potential too. Just be sure when picking an affiliate or network to represent that it has a good track record for product support and payment. You don't want to be associated with a bad product or worse yet, have all your promotional work to go to waste and wind up never getting paid.

Some of the top affiliate networks are:

CJ.com

clickbank.com

Amazon.com

eBay.com

This is just a short list. <u>If you'd like to see a few more click here</u>

There are literally hundreds, if not thousands of others. Again, just be sure to do your homework before getting involved with any company. Your livelihood depends on knowing who you are doing business with.

Where To Go From Here

I remember years ago when I got into internet marketing. I was overwhelmed by the sheer volume of information that I had to absorb. It seemed insurmountable! I quickly learned to take all these ideas in smaller chunks, implementing them one at a time. Which is why I wrote this book the way I did.

"*The journey of a thousand miles begins the first step*" in the famous saying goes. There's no right or wrong way to get started but the most you *can do* is to actually do it! Start at the beginning of this book and work your way through each of the ideas. Put them to use and test the results (measured in traffic and sales - that's the only *true* way that matters).

Spend each day taking another step and building another skill. I've been at this since 1992 and when I look back at all I have learned and accomplished since then I'm blown away by how much I've learned and managed to do with my daily addition of knowledge!

Now it the time to take *your* first steps.

Until next time,

Live Blessed!
Danial Barron Howe

For more great advice be sure to visit us

@

www.FiverrPowerTips.Com

See more recent titles from us

33 Fiverr Power Tips

Power Profits! Cash Flow Revolution

63 Ways to DRIVE MORE TRAFFIC to your website

101 TOTALLY FREE ways to market your website or blog

How To Build a YouTube Money Machine

The 10 Principles of ENDLESS WEALTH

For our full catalog visit us at:
2ndEmpireMedia.Com